Welcome to Your Coloring Adventure!

Welcome to a fun-filled adventure across Texas with Scout and Summit! This coloring book invites young explorers to travel across the Lone Star State alongside two curious friends as they discover the amazing places that make Texas special.

Inside, you'll find coloring pages inspired by Texas State Parks, historic sites, wildlife, and iconic Texas landscapes. From bluebonnet fields and sandy beaches to forests, deserts, and winding rivers, every page is a new place for Scout and Summit to explore.

Grab your crayons, markers, or colored pencils and bring each adventure to life. There's no right or wrong way to color—just have fun, be creative, and imagine what it would be like to explore these places yourself. Whether you've already visited these parks or are discovering them for the first time, we hope this book inspires curiosity, creativity, and a love for the great outdoors.

Join the Community!
Want to connect with other park lovers?

Join us on Instagram
@wanderstamped

Tag us & share photos, tips, coloring pages, and trip recommendations with fellow adventurers across the state. We'd love to see where your journey takes you!

See you on the trails, and happy exploring!

-The Wander Stamped Family

Scout & Summit Adventures: Texas Coloring Book
© 2026 Wander Stamped
All rights reserved.

For inquiries or permissions, contact:
Wander Stamped
wanderstamped@gmail.com

Printed in the United States of America.
First Edition: March 2026
ISBN: 979-8-9933698-7-7

Scout & Summit
Adventures: Texas

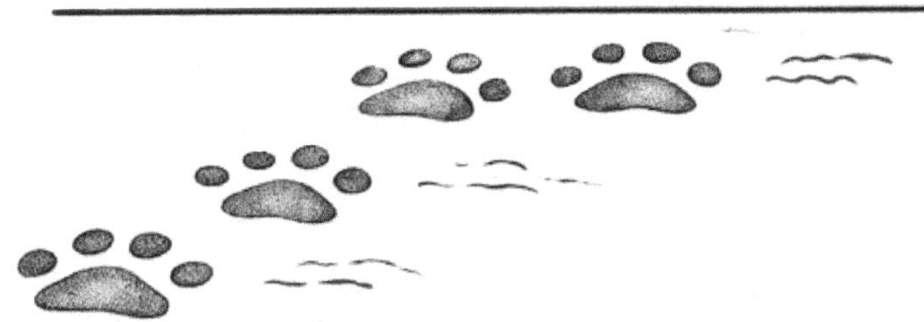

This book belongs to:

____

Howdy Texas!

Welcome to Texas
Drive Friendly – The Texas Way

40

44

ENCHANTED ROCK

56

Scout & Summit

Howdy from TEXAS!
Scout & Summit